CAT FARTS

COLORING BOOK

BELONGS TO:

Welcome to this cat World!

Find stunning types cats that fascinate young and old, but these farting ones will truly be a great anecdote as long as you enjoy painting them. Kittens purring out in the kitchen, bathroom, living room, desk, etc. really funny!

At FUN INNOVATIONS we have made an effort to create original drawings that you will surely enjoy!

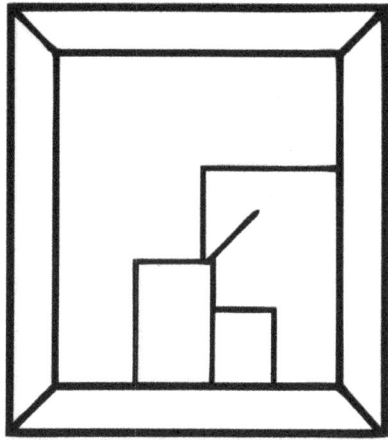

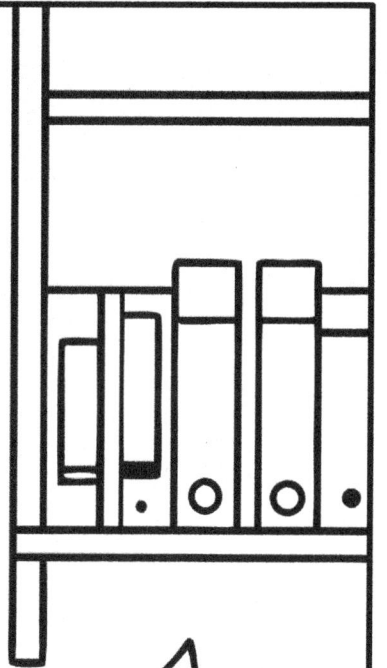

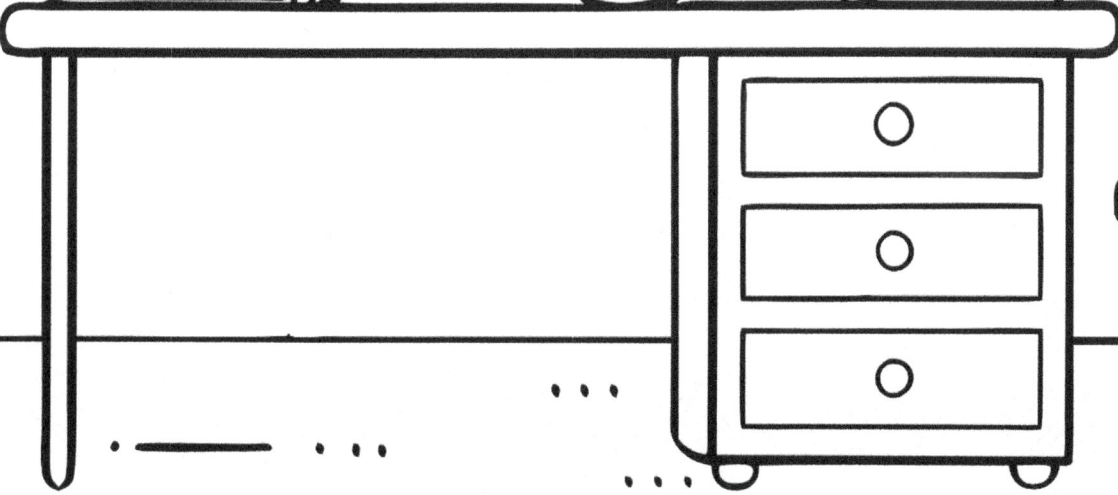

Thank you very much for buying this book!

If you enjoyed these drawings of cats farting for coloring, we would appreciate it if you could evaluate your purchase through a review.

At FUN INNOVATIONS we will always strive to improve. Stay tuned for more fun posts coming soon!.

Made in the USA
Las Vegas, NV
01 February 2025